Weather

by Sally Hewitt

amicus

Published by Amicus
P.O. Box 1329, Mankato, Minnesota 56002

Printed in the United States of America at Corporate
Graphics, in North Mankato, Minnesota.

Published by arrangement with the Watts Publishing
Group Ltd., London.

Library of Congress Cataloging-in-Publication Data

Hewitt, Sally, 1949-
  Weather / by Sally Hewitt.
    p. cm. -- (Starting geography)
  Summary: "Describes what weather is, how it affects
humans, tools to analyze weather, and different climates
around the world. Also describes the water cycle.
Includes hands-on activities"--Provided by publisher.
  Includes index.
  ISBN 978-1-60753-130-2 (lib. bdg.)
  1. Weather--Juvenile literature. I. Title.
  QC981.3.H482 2011
  551.6--dc22
                                            2009053181

Editor: Katie Dicker
Art Direction: Rahul Dhiman (Q2AMedia)
Designer: Shruti Aggarwal (Q2AMedia)
Picture researcher: Jyoti Seth (Q2AMedia)
Craft models made by: Tarang Saggar (Q2AMedia)
Photography: Divij Singh (Q2AMedia)

1211
32010

9 8 7 6 5 4 3 2 1

Picture credits:
t=top b=bottom c=center l=left r=right

Cover: Angelo Cavalli/Photolibrary
Title page: Dainis Derics/Istockphoto
Insides: Inc Superstock/Photolibrary: 6t,
Istockphoto: 6b, Shutterstock: 7, Maria
Yfanti/Shutterstock: 9l, Dvirus/Shutterstock: 9c,
Nata-Art /Shutterstock: 9r, Andreas
Weber/Dreamstime: 10t, Alexey Stiop/
Istockphoto: 10b, Kurt De Bruyn/Shutterstock: 12t,
Arturo Limon/Istockphoto: 12b, J-C&D. Pratt/
Photolibrary: 14b, Allar Bernard/Istockphoto: 16t,
Masterfile: 16b, Caroline Penn/Photolibrary: 18,
Dainis Derics/Istockphoto: 19, Phil
Degginger/Alamy: 20t, Eddie Gerald/Alamy: 20b,
Garnham Photography/ Istockphoto: 22t, Mark
Henley/Photolibrary: 22b, Adisa/Shutterstock: 23tc,
Roman Sigaev/Shutterstock: 23tl, Angelo
Gilardelli/Shutterstock: 23tr, Shutterstock: 23cl,
Cheryl Casey/Shutterstock: 23cr, Hasan Kursad
Ergan/Istockphoto: 23bl, Ryan Klos/Istockphoto:
23br, Christian Arnal/Photolibrary: 24t, Masterfile:
24b, William Casey/Istockphoto: 26, CC.
Lockwood/Photolibrary: 27t, Ramon Berk/
Shutterstock: 27b.

Q2AMedia Image Bank: Contents page, 11, 13,
15, 17, 19, 21, 25.
Q2AMedia Art Bank: Imprint page, 8, 14.

With thanks to our model Shruti Aggarwal.

Contents

Words that appear in **bold** can be found in the glossary on pages 28–29.

What Is Weather?

Weather is what is happening in the air outside. Weather is how hot or cold the air feels, how much the air is moving, and how much water is in the air.

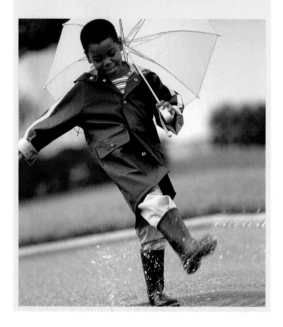
When we go outside, we dress for the weather.

Why Is Weather Important?

Weather affects us in all kinds of ways. Too much rain can bring **floods** and not enough rain can cause **droughts**. Warm, sunny days are perfect for camping, but high winds will blow the tents away! A weather **forecast** tells us what type of weather to expect.

Climate

Each area in the world has a particular type of weather pattern over a period of time. This is called the **climate**. Over millions of years, plants, animals, and people **adapt** to survive the climate of their area.

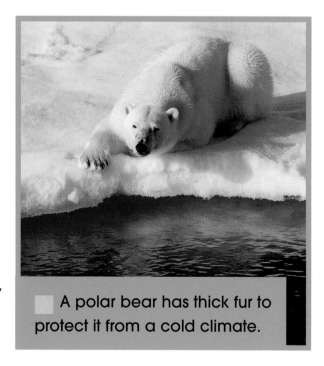
A polar bear has thick fur to protect it from a cold climate.

Climate Zones

The world is divided into five **climate zones**. The polar zone is always cold, snowy, and icy. The cold zone has short, cool summers and long, cold winters. The temperate zone has cool winters and warm summers. In the dry zone, there is hardly any rain. The days are very hot, and the nights are cold. The tropical zone is hot and wet all year round.

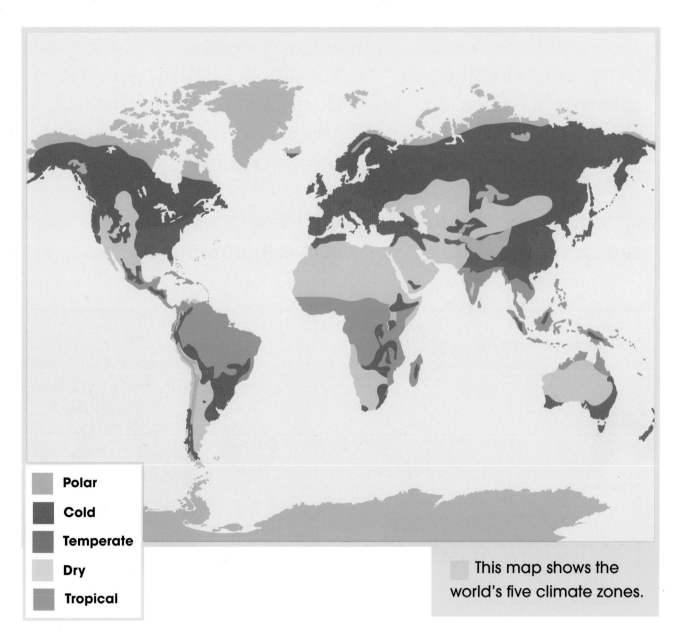

Polar

Cold

Temperate

Dry

Tropical

This map shows the world's five climate zones.

Temperature

The temperature is how hot or cold the air is outside. The sun gives planet Earth its heat. As the Earth moves around the sun and clouds fill the sky, the temperature changes.

Seasons

The Earth takes a year to move around the sun, spinning as it goes. It is tilted, so the top of the Earth points away or toward the sun at different stages of its journey. This causes the **seasons** to change.

Changes in Temperature

During the day, the sun warms the ground, which heats the air above it. At night, the ground and the air cool down. The air also cools when the sun goes behind a cloud. We measure temperature with a **thermometer**.

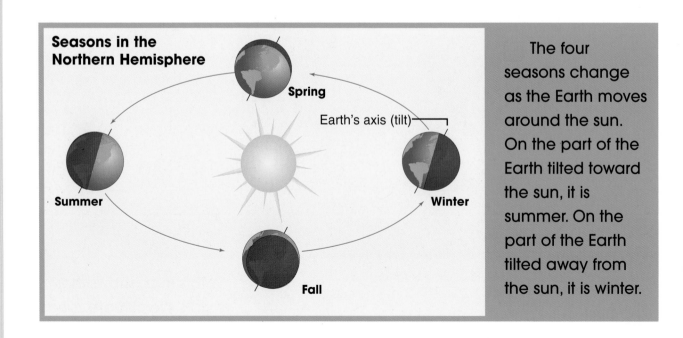

Seasons in the Northern Hemisphere

Spring

Earth's axis (tilt)

Summer

Winter

Fall

The four seasons change as the Earth moves around the sun. On the part of the Earth tilted toward the sun, it is summer. On the part of the Earth tilted away from the sun, it is winter.

Make a Temperature Chart

You will need:
- 2 garden thermometers (from a garden center)
- notebook • sheet of card stock • pencil and markers • ruler

1 Outside, hang one thermometer in a sunny place and the other nearby but in a shady place.

2 On the card stock, make a chart like the one below. Record the temperature in the sunny and shady places at the same time of day for a week. Mark your temperature and weather data on the chart.

	Mon	Tues	Wed	Thurs	Fri
Weather	☀	⛅	☁	🌧	☁
Temp 1 Sunny Spot	71°F/ 22°C	64°F/ 18°C	59°F/ 15°C	61°F/ 16°C	57°F/ 14°C
Temp 2 Shady Spot	64°F/ 18°C	59°F/ 15°C	57°F/ 14°C	59°F/ 15°C	55°F/ 13°C

What do you notice about the temperature changes in the different places?

Atmosphere

Our planet is surrounded by a mixture of gases, dust, and **water vapor** that make up the **atmosphere**. The atmosphere protects the Earth from the sun's heat and stops warmth from escaping into space.

Airplanes fly above the clouds where the air is thin and the weather is calmer. This gives a smoother ride.

Thick and Thin Air

The mixture of gases in the atmosphere is called air. Air is thickest and heaviest near the ground. The sun warms this thicker air and causes it to move as wind. Air spreads out when it rises, so the air becomes thinner higher up.

Air Pressure

Even though we can't feel it, air presses down on us all the time. This is called air pressure. When air falls and warms, causing high pressure, calm sunny weather is on the way. When air rises and cools, with low pressure, it may bring wet and windy weather.

Air pressure is measured with a barometer.

Make a Simple Barometer

You will need:
- card stock • scissors markers • tape • straight drinking straw • large jar
- balloon • rubber band

1 Cut a strip of card stock about 12 in. (30 cm) long and 2 in. (5 cm) wide. Draw a sun at the top and gray clouds at the bottom.

2 Make a pointer by cutting a small arrow from the card stock and tape it to one end of the straw.

3 Put the jar on a shelf or windowsill and balance the pointer across the top of the jar. Prop the card stock up so that the arrow points to the middle of the card. Mark the middle with a line.

4 Cut the neck end off the balloon. Stretch the balloon over the open top of the jar so it is stretched tight and smooth. Secure the balloon with the rubber band. Make sure the jar is airtight.

5 Tape the straw to the middle of the stretched balloon. About 3/4 of the straw should stick out.

6 Put your barometer back on the shelf with the pointer pointing at the card stock. High air pressure pushes down on the balloon and the pointer rises above the line. Low air pressure pushes less on the balloon, and the pointer falls below the line.

Wind

Wind is moving air. We can't see wind, but we can feel it as it blows on our skin and hair. We can also see things moving as wind blows against them.

Moving Air

Changes in air pressure keep the air moving. This creates wind. Wind blows from areas of high pressure to areas of low pressure. **Global winds** sweep around the whole Earth. Global westerly winds blow the weather from west to east across North America.

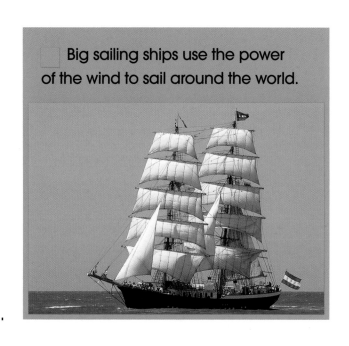

Big sailing ships use the power of the wind to sail around the world.

The cups of an anemometer turn to show the speed of the wind.

Speed and Direction

It can be important to know the speed and direction of the wind. High winds are dangerous for **construction** workers on tall buildings. Strong winds can blow an airplane off course or affect an athlete in a race. Wind speed and direction is measured by an **anemometer**.

Make a Cup Anemometer

Ask an adult to help you with this activity.

You will need:
- 2 straight drinking straws
- tape • 4 small paper cups
- stapler • thumb tack
- sharp pencil with an eraser

1 Lay the drinking straws so they cross at the center. Tape them together where they cross.

3 Staple the ends of the straws to the tops of the cups near the rims.

4 Ask an adult to push a thumb tack through the center of the straws and into the pencil eraser. Hold the pencil, and blow into the cups to see if your anemometer spins freely.

2 Place a paper cup sideways at both ends of each straw. Make sure they are all pointing in the same direction.

Use the anemometer outside to test the speed and strength of the wind. The cups spin quickly in a high wind and slowly in a breeze.

Water

Water goes around and around among land, sea, and sky in a circle called the **water cycle**. The water cycle keeps water on the move and changes the weather.

Water Cycle

When the sun heats water on Earth, some of the water evaporates into the air as water vapor. As it rises, it cools and turns to water drops that form clouds. The water falls back to Earth as rain, sleet, hail, or snow. This is called precipitation.

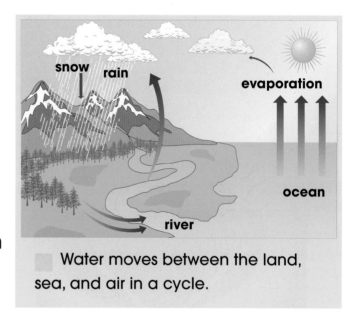

snow   rain

evaporation

ocean

river

Water moves between the land, sea, and air in a cycle.

Clouds can tell us what type of weather is coming.

Clouds and Precipitation

Clouds form at different levels in the air. Small, white, puffy clouds come with sunny weather. High, wispy clouds tell us sunny weather will change. Towering, dark clouds bring storms and heavy rain or hail. Low layers of gray clouds bring rain, sleet, or snow.

Make a Water Cycle Circle

Ask an adult to help you with this activity.

You will need:
- 2 large circles of cardboard
- pencil • ruler • markers
- card stock • scissors
- tape • paper fastener

1 Use the pencil and ruler to divide one circle into six equal segments.

2 Copy the template below to draw the stages of the water cycle in each segment. Label each segment and color the pictures.

3 Take the second circle of cardboard and ask an adult to help you cut a window in the shape of a water drop. It should be big enough to reveal one segment of the first circle. Stick a small cardboard tab next to the window.

4 Ask an adult to fasten the circles together at the center with the paper fastener. Hold the tab and turn the wheel in a clockwise direction to show water going through the water cycle.

Storm!

A storm is a violent weather event. A storm can have strong winds, heavy rain and hail, blinding snow, thunder and lightning, or swirling sands. Storms often cause great damage.

Thunder and Lightning

When giant clouds grow like dark towers in the sky on a hot, damp day, a thunderstorm could be on its way. Lightning is caused by huge sparks of **electricity** flashing between storm clouds and the ground. It can set fire to trees.

You should stay indoors during a fierce thunderstorm, away from the lightning.

In the U.S., there are about 1,000 tornadoes every year.

Hurricanes and Tornadoes

Hurricanes are huge, swirling masses of wind and rain. They form over the sea and move inland where they can cause terrible damage. A **tornado** is a twisting funnel of air from a storm cloud to the ground. Tornadoes are so strong that they can pick up trucks in their path.

Tornado Trick

Ask an adult to help you with this activity.

Amaze your friends by making a tornado in a bottle.

You will need:
- 2 large plastic bottles
- duct tape • sharp pencil
- jug of water

1 Take the lids off the bottles. Cover the spout of one of the bottles with duct tape. Make sure it is watertight.

2 Ask an adult to use the pencil to make a hole (a bit bigger than a hole punch) in the center of the duct tape over the spout.

3 Fill the other bottle 3/4 full of water and turn the empty bottle upside down on top of it. Tape the two bottles together and check for leaks.

4 Turn the bottles so the bottle with water is on the top. Swirl the bottles gently and watch the water form a water tornado effect in the top bottle, with a tube of air running through the middle of it.

Extreme Weather

When certain types of weather come together at once, they can form extreme weather conditions. Extreme weather can be very dangerous for people, animals, and plants.

Floods and Drought

Rain doesn't fall evenly all over the Earth. Some areas have very little rain, while others have rain most days. When there is too much rain, rivers can flood, destroying crops and making water dirty and dangerous to drink. Too little rain causes a drought. Crops die and people become hungry and thirsty.

These women in Eritrea, Africa, are waiting to collect water from a well during a drought.

Extreme Hot and Cold

A heat wave happens when the land and air heat up and the temperature becomes unusually high. In freezing temperatures, rain can turn to hail, sleet, or snow. High winds whip snow into a blizzard.

Swirling snow in a blizzard makes it difficult to see.

Make Some Snowflakes

Every snowflake is different, but they all have six points.

You will need:
- squares of white paper (of different sizes) • pencil
- scissors • glue • large sheet of dark blue paper • glitter

1 Fold the squares in half and then in half again to make smaller squares.

2 Find the corner that is the center of the square when it is opened.

Turn the folded square so this corner is bottom left.

3 Copy the snowflake shape shown in the template and cut it out along the black lines. Try some shapes of your own on the other squares.

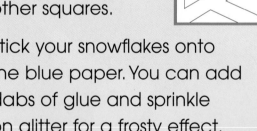
Template

4 Stick your snowflakes onto the blue paper. You can add dabs of glue and sprinkle on glitter for a frosty effect.

Weather Forecasting

Weather forecasting gives us information about what weather we can expect. Knowing what the weather is going to be like helps us to plan a day out.

Weather Check

The weather is constantly checked around the world. **Satellites** above the Earth collect information about the weather from space. This information is sent to computers to help weather forecasters predict the weather ahead.

A weather satellite takes photographs and measures the temperature on Earth.

This map shows the weather forecast for North America.

Charts and Symbols

Weather forecasters prepare charts with **symbols** for television, radio, newspapers, and the Internet. They show us what weather to expect in the next few hours or days in a particular area. They have a difficult job because the weather is always changing.

Make Your Own Weather Station

Ask an adult to help you with this activity.

Make your own weather station. Use your barometer, anemometer, and thermometer, and add a rain gauge.

You will need:
- large plastic bottle
- duct tape • ruler
- waterproof marker

1 Ask an adult to cut the top third off the bottle. Turn the top of the bottle upside down. Put it into the bottom of the bottle to make a funnel. Tape around the top with duct tape.

2 Stick a strip of tape up the side of the bottle. Use the ruler and waterproof

marker to write on a scale in inches/cm from the bottom to the top of the tape.

3 Place your rain gauge outside in the open. You could wedge it between stones to stop it from blowing away.

4 At the same time each day, record the amount of water collected in the bottle. Then empty it. Check the air pressure, wind speed, and temperature, too. Record your findings on a chart. Can you use your results to predict the weather?

	Mon	Tues	Wed	Thurs	Fri
Amount of rain	1 in. (2.5 cm)	0 in. (0 cm)	0.5 in. (1.3 cm)	0 in. (0 cm)	1 in. (2.5 cm)
Air pressure	low	low	low	medium	low
Wind speed	medium	low	medium	low	medium
Temperature	61°F/ 16°C	59°F/ 15°C	61°F/ 16°C	63°F/ 17°C	61°F/ 16°C

Weather and Lifestyles

The type of weather in a particular area affects the way people live there and the type of plants that grow. People often go on vacation to experience different weather.

The Mediterranean

The weather around the Mediterranean Sea is hot and dry in summer and warm and wet in winter. People spend lots of time outdoors. The weather is just right for farmers to grow fruit such as grapes, oranges, and lemons.

Lemons grow well in the Mediterranean climate.

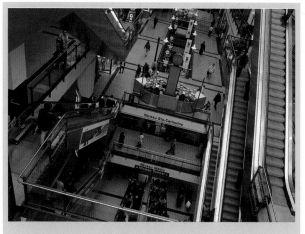
This shopping mall in Canada is linked to a subway station.

Cold Climate

In the cold climate of northern North America and northern Europe and Asia, the summers are short and cool, and the winters are long and cold. In some cities, shopping malls are underground. This helps people avoid the harsh winter weather.

Plan a Day Out

1 You are going on a class trip. Decide where you want to go—perhaps to the beach or the mountains. Find your destination on a map.

2 Find a weather forecast in a newspaper, on television, on the radio, or the Internet to find out what weather to expect.

www.forecast247.com

Weather Forecast

Home

Travel

Photos

Map

A warm start with a few showers. The afternoon will become brighter and mostly dry with sunny intervals.

3 How will the weather affect your plans?
a) What will you wear?
b) What activities will you do?
c) What equipment will you need?
d) How will you get there?

How will you alter your plans if the weather changes?

Adapting to Weather

The design of the houses people live in, the clothes they wear, what they eat and drink, and the jobs they do are all affected by the local weather.

Jobs and Tourism

Where there is warm sunshine, tourists come to sunbathe and swim. People work in the mornings and evenings and rest in the heat of the day. Where there is plenty of snow in winter, people enjoy sports such as skiing and sledding.

Some local people in the mountains work as ski instructors.

In Japan, paper parasols help to shade people from the hot sun.

Houses and Clothes

Where it is cold all year round, houses have sloping roofs for the snow to slide off. People keep themselves warm by wearing thick clothes. In a hot, dry climate, houses have small windows to keep out the sun. People prefer to wear loose, light clothes.

Make a Japanese Parasol

Ask an adult to help you with this activity.

You will need:
- markers • large and small circle of thick colored paper 8 in. (20 cm) across and 3 in. (8 cm) across • sharp pencil
- ruler • scissors • bead
- thin stick, 8 in. (20 cm) long
- glue • poster putty

1 Use the markers to decorate the large circle. Draw a line from the side to the center of the circle and cut along it.

2 Fold a section of the circle so it is pointed at the center and about 0.5 in. (1.5 cm) wide at the edge. Make repeated folds back and forth all the way round the circle as if you were making a fan.

3 Stick the first and last folds together to make the shape of your parasol shade.

4 Ask an adult to use the pencil to make a small hole in the center of both circles. Push the stick through the hole in the parasol shade. Glue the bead to the top of the stick.

5 Press poster putty around the stick beneath the parasol shade to hold it in place. Push the small circle up to the top of the stick to open the parasol. Pull it down to close it again.

Changing Climates

The climate on our planet has been changing very gradually over millions of years. Now it is changing more quickly because of things people are doing all over the world.

Global Warming

Fumes from **exhaust pipes**, factory chimneys, and power plants send gases into the air. They are called **greenhouse gases** because they trap the heat of the sun, like the glass in a greenhouse. These gases contribute to rising temperatures on Earth. We call this **global warming**.

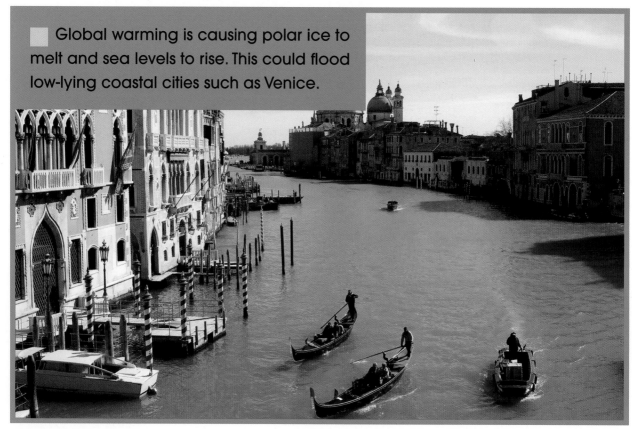

Global warming is causing polar ice to melt and sea levels to rise. This could flood low-lying coastal cities such as Venice.

Extreme Weather

If global warming continues, we should expect more extreme weather events in the future. There will probably be less cold and frost in some places and more heat waves and drought in others. Heavier rain will bring more floods and there may be more storms.

Climate change could mean more storms like Hurricane Katrina that flooded New Orleans in 2005.

Write a Newspaper Report

Research a recent extreme weather event using books or the Internet and write a short newspaper article about a similar imaginary event.

a) Describe the weather as it happened.

b) Quote an eye-witness account.

c) Describe what the place looked like after the event was over.

d) What damage was done?

e) What kind of help did the local people need?

Glossary

adapt

Plants, animals, and people that adapt have changed over time to survive in their environment.

anemometer

An anemometer is an instrument that measures the speed and direction of the wind.

atmosphere

The atmosphere is the mixture of gases, dust, and water vapor that surrounds the Earth.

climate

Climate is the type of weather a place has over a long time.

climate zone

A climate zone is a large area that has a particular type of climate.

construction

Construction is the making or building of something.

drought

A drought is a long period of very dry weather when there is not enough rain for crops to grow.

electricity

Electricity is a type of energy. Lightning is a form of electricity.

exhaust pipe

An exhaust pipe is a pipe fitted to a vehicle through which fumes from burning fuel escape.

floods

Floods are caused when rivers become too full and overflow.

forecast

A forecast is a prediction of what might happen in the future, such as a change in the weather.

global warming

Global warming is the gradual increase of the world's temperature. It is partly caused by greenhouse gases in the air.

global winds

Global winds are winds that blow in one direction for long distances around the Earth.

greenhouse gas

A greenhouse gas is a type of gas that traps heat from the sun. Carbon dioxide is one example.

hurricane

A hurricane is a very powerful tropical storm with high winds and heavy rain.

satellite

A satellite is a spacecraft that goes around the Earth. Weather satellites send information about the weather from space back to Earth.

season

A season is a period of a particular type of weather. The year is divided into four seasons—spring, summer, fall, and winter.

symbol

A symbol is a simple picture that stands for something. For example, the symbol for snow could be a snowflake.

thermometer

A thermometer is an instrument that measures the temperature of air or water, for example.

tornado

A tornado is a type of windstorm in the form of a funnel of air that spins over land.

water cycle

The water cycle is the movement of water around and around among air, sea, and land. Rain falls to the ground and runs into rivers and the sea. Water evaporates into clouds and falls again as rain, sleet, or snow.

water vapor

Water vapor is formed when liquid water turns into a gas.

Index